MW01056531

THE STORY OF ME AND MY GRANDMA

Life Canvas:

First published by Parragon Books Ltd in 2013
LIFE CANVAS is an imprint of Parragon Books Ltd

Parragon
Chartist House
15-17 Trim Street
Bath BA1 1HA, UK
www.parragon.com

Produced by Tall Tree Ltd
Illustrations by Apple Agency

ISBN 978-1-4723-0744-6
GTIN 5060292801049

Printed in China

I made this book for my
Grandma because...

love from...

where ....

when ....

Here's a photo
OF ME AND YOU

OUR JOURNEY TOGETHER

If you follow this thread through the book, you'll see photos, some old and some new, to make up a timeline of the things we've done together over the years.

stick your photo here

THESE ARE A FEW OF YOUR FAVORITE THINGS

and a few of mine too!

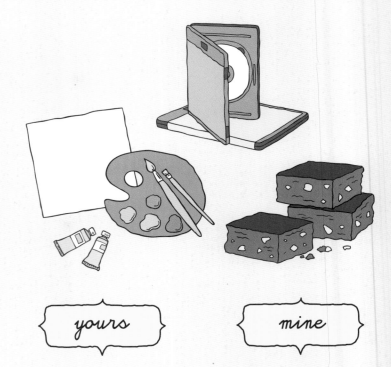

	yours	mine
Favorite **TV** show		
Favorite song		
Favorite color		
Favorite food		
Favorite snack		
Favorite movie		
Favorite hobby		
Favorite sport		
Favorite book		

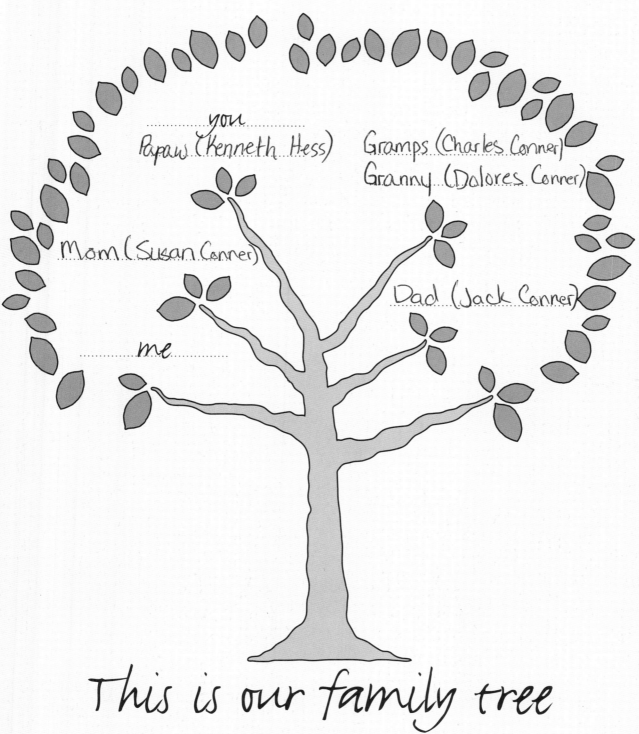

you
Papaw (Kenneth Hess)

Gramps (Charles Conner)
Granny (Dolores Conner)

Mom (Susan Conner)

Dad (Jack Conner)

me

This is our family tree

Fill in the blanks with your grandparents and
parents to make your family tree.

I MAKE THESE FACES WHEN

Grandma makes these dishes

Spaghetti and meatballs 😄 🙂 😐 🙁

Liver and onions 😄 🙂 😐 🙁

Scrambled eggs 😄 🙂 😐 🙁

Cheesecake 😄 🙂 😐 🙁

Broccoli 😄 🙂 😐 🙁

Apple pie 😄 🙂 😐 🙁

Chocolate cake 😄 🙂 😐 🙁

.... 😄 🙂 😐 🙁

.... 😄 🙂 😐 🙁

.... 😄 🙂 😐 🙁

.... 😄 🙂 😐 🙁

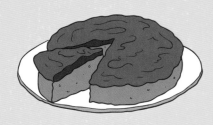

Thoughtful

Silly

Generous

Creative

Kind

A pie of your personality!

Funny

Fun

Smart

Caring

Cheerful

Strict

Stubborn

Look at these words: think of Grandma and what she's like, and divide the
pie into the different characteristics that make up her personality.

YOU, ME, AND ....

A photo of three generations of our family.

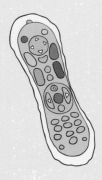

I'll show you how to

1. ....

2. ....

3. ....

4. ....

5. ....

6. ....

... and you can show me

1. ....

2. ....

3. ....

4. ....

5. ....

6. ....

SWAPPING SKILLS

stick your photo here

At Grandma's house
YOU'LL ALWAYS FIND

- [ ] Books to read
- [ ] Craft projects
- [ ] Leftovers
- [ ] Embarrassing photos of Mom/Dad
- [ ] Stories from long ago
- [ ] Someone to laugh with
- [ ] Old magazines
- [ ] Music playing
- [ ] The TV on
- [ ] Candy
- [ ] ....
- [ ] ....
- [ ] ....

Whenever I stay
with Grandma, we
do these things

IF I COOKED GRANDMA'S ☰FAVORITE FOOD☰ I'D MAKE HER...

Appetizer

Main course

Dessert

Delivery available • Service not included • Private parties catered for

GRANDMA LIKES*

	really likes	likes	doesn't mind	dislikes
Gardening	☐	☐	☐	☐
Shopping	☐	☐	☐	☐
Watching me	☐	☐	☐	☐
Doing crossword puzzles	☐	☐	☐	☐
Laundry	☐	☐	☐	☐
Cooking	☐	☐	☐	☐
Dancing	☐	☐	☐	☐
Working	☐	☐	☐	☐
Crafting	☐	☐	☐	☐
Reading	☐	☐	☐	☐
Watching TV	☐	☐	☐	☐
Playing computer games	☐	☐	☐	☐
Meeting friends	☐	☐	☐	☐
Going out for lunch	☐	☐	☐	☐
....	☐	☐	☐	☐
....	☐	☐	☐	☐
....	☐	☐	☐	☐
....	☐	☐	☐	☐

*OR DOES SHE?

Grandma's best hints for a MIDNIGHT SNACK

1. ....
2. ....
3. ....
4. ....
5. ....

stick your photo here

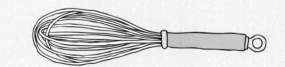

GRANDMA
MAKES THE BEST

and this is her recipe

We nearly got into
TROUBLE WHEN...

We had a great vacation
WHEN WE WENT TO...

....
....
....
....
....
....
....

stick your photo here

GRANDMA'S
magic cures

Problem	Cure
1.	1.
2.	2.
3.	3.
4.	4.
5.	5.

I WISH I'D TAKEN A
PHOTO WHEN

Write or draw a picture in the space above of something Grandma did.

HOW GOOD
ARE YOU AT?

Color the stars from left to right.

Cooking	☆	☆	☆	☆	☆	☆	☆	☆
Playing board games	☆	☆	☆	☆	☆	☆	☆	☆
Singing	☆	☆	☆	☆	☆	☆	☆	☆
Talking on the phone	☆	☆	☆	☆	☆	☆	☆	☆
Doing puzzles	☆	☆	☆	☆	☆	☆	☆	☆
Playing tennis	☆	☆	☆	☆	☆	☆	☆	☆
Bike riding	☆	☆	☆	☆	☆	☆	☆	☆
Telling stories	☆	☆	☆	☆	☆	☆	☆	☆
Drawing	☆	☆	☆	☆	☆	☆	☆	☆
Playing computer games	☆	☆	☆	☆	☆	☆	☆	☆
Growing flowers	☆	☆	☆	☆	☆	☆	☆	☆

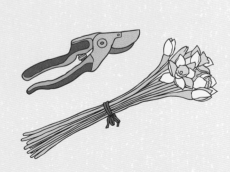

stick your photo here

Grandma always says

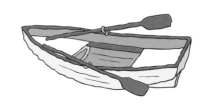

OF ALL THE STORIES YOU'VE *ever told me,* THIS ONE IS MY **FAVORITE**

Giggle GRAPH

Create a bar chart of things that make Grandma laugh.

ROFL
(Roll on Floor Laughing)

LOL

Quiet laugh

Giggle

Grin

Smile

Grandpa's jokes

The best things Grandma
EVER MADE FOR ME

....

....

....

....

....

....

Things I *love* to do with *you*

1. ....

2. ....

3. ....

4. ....

5. ....

6. ....

Grandma
loves to sing these songs

1. ....
2. ....
3. ....
4. ....
5. ....

and I like to sing
these songs

1. ....
2. ....
3. ....
4. ....
5. ....

stick your photo here

YOU SAY I'M LIKE MY MOM/DAD BECAUSE...

Grandma's
PET PEEVES ARE...

Caught on camera
doing something silly!

A perfect day spent with you

GRANDMA'S SCORECARD

Sense of humor	1 2 3 4 5 6 7 8 9 10
Driving skills	1 2 3 4 5 6 7 8 9 10
Taste in TV shows	1 2 3 4 5 6 7 8 9 10
Spoiling me	1 2 3 4 5 6 7 8 9 10
Shopping for bargains	1 2 3 4 5 6 7 8 9 10
Keeping secrets	1 2 3 4 5 6 7 8 9 10
Listening	1 2 3 4 5 6 7 8 9 10

Circle Grandma's marks out of ten.

Grandma's
favorite things to do on a
summer's day

....
....
....
....
....
....
....
....
....
....
....
....
....
....
....
....
....
....

stick your photo here

Played these sports ....

Read these books ....

Watched these movies ....

Gone to these places ....

Worn these clothes ....

When you were my age
I THINK YOU
WOULD HAVE

YOU TAUGHT ME

How to play ....

How to make ....

Who .... was

Where to buy ....

How to surf the
Internet for ....

AND I TAUGHT YOU

How to play ....

How to make ....

Who .... was

Where to buy ....

How to surf the
Internet for ....

Grandma's
favorite
TV characters

1. ....
2. ....
3. ....
4. ....

1. ....
2. ....
3. ....
4. ....

And my
favorite
TV characters

It was really fun when we went to...

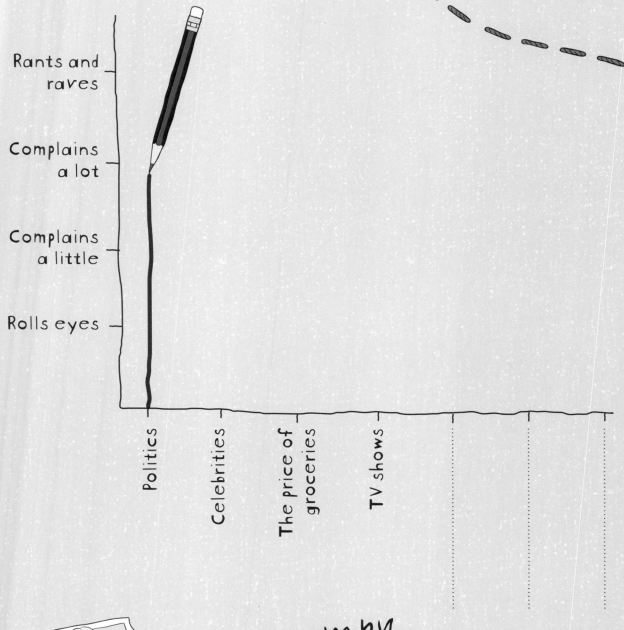

Rants and raves

Complains a lot

Complains a little

Rolls eyes

Politics

Celebrities

The price of groceries

TV shows

Grumpy GRAPH

Complete this line graph to see how grumpy Grandma is.

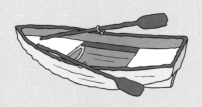

....
....
....
....
....
....
....
....
....
....
....
....
....
....
....
....

I REMEMBER
WHEN WE

We still need to do these things together

1. ....
2. ....
3. ....
4. ....
5. ....

stick your photo here

I hope when i'm older, i am more like you in these ways:

....
....
....
....
....
....

stick your photo here

Things I admire in
GRANDMA

FIVE THINGS

1. ....
2. ....
3. ....
4. ....
5. ....

I'D WISH FOR YOU

why you mean
THE WORLD
TO ME

YOU AND ME NOW

WORLD'S NICEST

YOU'RE THE BEST

MY COOL GRANDMA

BEST GRANDMA

My Grandma

SUPER-GRANDMA

I LOVE YOU GRANDMA

WORLD'S BEST GRANDMA

Let's play · Let's bake · Time for a treat · Fixed by Grandma

Let's play · Let's bake · Time for a treat · Fixed by Grandma